This book belongs to:

_____

Other books include:
My Mindfulness Guide - Sixty Days of Self Reflection

Disclaimer

Guided writing is a healthy practice to add to your daily routine. While it can enhance your overall health and wellbeing, it's not meant to replace other necessary lifestyle practices such as proper nutrition, regular exercise and quality sleep. We always encourage you to seek additional professional support should life's challenges become overwhelming or too difficult to deal with on your own. Please consult your doctor or physical before embarking on physical activity.

©2019 Jen CB | My Grieving Guide
All content contained herein is copyright of Jen CB, absolutely no reproduction or distribution permitted. Inquiries may be addressed to info@jencb.com.
This edition was designed and produced in Barrie, Ontario. Every effort has been made to ensure the accuracy of the information presented, however, we cannot be held liable for any errors, omissions or inconsistencies.

Introduction

A widow falls to the kitchen floor in tears. Only a week ago she called 911, as her husband was experiencing unusual flu-like symptoms. Little did she know that it was stage 4 of pancreatic cancer, eating him from the inside out. In those moments on the cold kitchen floor, not knowing what her future would hold, she screamed out loud in anguish. Her dogs watched helplessly as tears rolled down her face. Alone with only her thoughts, the sound of silence echoed through the house in a haunting manner.

Her husband used to watch TV downstairs on a Sunday afternoon, and she recalled hearing his footsteps coming up the stairs every now and then to check on her. No longer is the TV on, nor the sound of footsteps other than her slow pace as she walks around the house mumbling to herself, "I can't believe you are gone". How can one cope with these trials and tribulations of grief? She doesn't want to be seen right now. She doesn't have the energy to leave the house. How can she move forward and get on with her life?

Life can change in a matter of moments for an individual. The sudden loss of a loved one, a pet, a job, can be traumatizing and the emotions of sorrow and despair can be overwhelming. Moments of fatigue, helplessness, loneliness, even anger, all affect our mental state. Sometimes an informal way of learning can prove to be most beneficial to those experiencing the grief-stricken sorrow that can take over your entire life. Your thoughts become cloudy, your decision making becomes muddled and you feel so confused. Sound familiar?

Over the last 20 years of practicing mindfulness to enhance different areas of my life, I'm here to encourage and teach you to develop a practice to strengthen your mind and have a deeper connection with your soul's purpose. As I will address in "the problem" section, we live in a culture where we are deeply distracted. Currently, humans are being pushed, pulled, and expanded beyond our means. And where does this leave us for when we experience loss in life? Regardless if you have lost someone due to death, illness, loss of a friendship, loss of a job, or even anticipatory grief, these major shifts can wreak havoc on our health and wellbeing. As a result, we need to find ways to create a fundamental practice of mindfulness training in order to keep our minds, our bodies and our soul's purpose in line and in balance moving forward along our path. Like an athlete who works on fundamental skills training, mindfulness training provides different fundamentals to help individuals become more involved in the present and help move those grief emotions through their body in a healthy manner.

This guide is designed to be a gentle read while guiding you through writing prompts to connect you to your thoughts and reflections. This helps process those grief stricken emotions in a calm way, so that you may heal along your path with more ease and grace. The inspiration behind this book is to give writing prompts in order to help you create, what I like to call, a "new normal" in your life. You are encouraged to become more aware of your mind, your heart centre, and your deep soul's purpose moving forward after experiencing a loss. You will notice a couple of small sections of reading and information for you, while a few sections are designed for you to write your thoughts, feelings, and emotions. This is because when we are in those deep feelings of grief, it is more difficult to retain information. Therefore a little bit of reading and a little bit of writing will help strengthen those neurotransmitters to help you to begin moving forward.

Through my own grief journey, I had writing guides everywhere in my house. Whenever I felt the waves of emotions, I turned to writing to help me process my thoughts and feelings in a healthy matter. What I noticed was how quickly my emotions came through me, feeling much like ocean waves. If I allowed my thoughts and feelings to flow out onto the paper, these waves seemed to pass quickly and I was able to move on with my day. If I suppressed these emotions, I felt like I was being sucked under from the undertow of my grief. I encourage my clients to *"ride the wave"*. This is where you are able to surf and rise above that undercurrent of emotions. I explain more of these feelings in the "How can we use mindfulness in our life after loss?" section on page 9.

I fully respect that every grief journey and each loss is different for everyone, at any given moment along their path. However, I wish you all the best on your writing journey in the days ahead, remember love and support is always around you to help you heal.

With Much Love,
JenCB

Defining Grief

Grief is defined as the emotional response in and thereafter the death of someone you love. It is known as the mental suffering or distress over a loss. Whether it is the death of a loved one, a pet, the loss of a job, the loss of a friendship, the emotions of grief can take its toll on anyone. Grief doesn't always have to be linked with death. Where should we reach out to? How do we heal from such a loss in our lives? Unlike mental or a physical illness, grief affects us all at one point in our lives or another. Grief is a deep emotional response to an intense loss of life and the symptoms can include loss of sleep, depression, excessive eating or drinking, antisocial behaviour, anger, sadness, loss of motivation, etc.

Grief is an umbrella term that is used to encompass loss, the emotions associated with loss and the mental state and emotional process you experience afterwards. Much research concludes that grief is as individual as our lives and therefore we should recognize that the healing process can differ from person to person. Grief is real because the loss is real and therefore dismissing this emotion is rather unhealthy. By writing out our emotions we can create a process in order to think clearly again. This is why I highly believe that mindfulness training can provide clarity in moments of chaos.

Grief is painful and can be very isolating. Therefore the question arises, how does one heal or obtain access to healing opportunities if the only thing they want to do is be alone? How can we address this and develop ways to enhance our fundamental skills of being in the moment and aware?

By practicing mindfulness skills (like journal or guided writing), we all have the capacity to develop a sense of calm and compassion that can help us handle difficult moments with greater equanimity. As a young widow, I turned to writing to help me through the dark moments of grief, loneliness, and despair. These steps were vital for me in order to put my life back together again and help me to create my "new normal". Writing gave me a sense of moving through the negative emotions, which helped me foster new ideas and a sense of wellbeing again. It took a while, but mindfulness writing became a process that when I used it consistently (along with seeking various forms of professional assistance), it helped me to find my way back to living a happy and joyous life again.

So let's begin with an understanding of Mindfulness Training. This section may be familiar if you have already read "My Mindfulness Guide". However, it is crucial to your writing journey, so I encourage you to read this section again to refresh your understanding of mindfulness right now, from the perspective of how it can help you through your grieving process.

What is Mindfulness?

Mindfulness training helps us become aware of our present state, improving our physical and mental capabilities, as they work together in a cohesive unit for optimal life performance. Much like the body, the mental state of awareness in an individual needs attention as well. Mindfulness training is a tool used in various holistic practices to improve optimum life performance. From yoga, meditation, and labyrinth experiences, the improvement of mental health has been a fundamental focus in recent years to help individuals, of all age groups, achieve optimum growth and development. Recently, mindfulness training has gained momentum as a viable alternative approach to prepare athletes (and other individuals) for optimal sport performance. From holistic practices, athletics, science and education, work-life balance, mindfulness meditation and training techniques have been utilized in many different areas to enhance an individual sense of self. When we are mindful of our thoughts, our bodies, our emotions; when we have the opportunity to be entirely concentrated on our mind, our body, our soul's purpose, we have the opportunity to achieve insight for our life's purpose and path.

Mindfulness means maintaining a moment-by-moment awareness of our thoughts, feelings, bodily sensations, and the surrounding environment without judging ourselves in that state of awareness. Mindfulness involves acceptance, meaning that we pay attention to our thoughts and feelings without judging them, without believing, for instance, that there's a "right" or "wrong" way to think or feel in a given moment. When we practice mindfulness, our thoughts tune into what we're sensing in the present moment rather than rehashing the past or imagining the future. With its roots in Buddhist meditation, a secular practice of mindfulness has entered the American/Canadian mainstream in recent years, in part through the work of Kabat-Zinn and his Mindfulness-Based Stress Reduction (MBSR) program, which he launched at the University of Massachusetts Medical School in 1979. The root of individual growth should be about the presence of heart and the emotional connection within the centre of your being.

I have broken down mindfulness training into a three step process. For this guide, I will also elaborate on how mindfulness writing can help assist you through your grief and steps to create your new normal.

The first step is **Self-Care**: This involves deep listening to your self. What do you need during this time in your life? Allow yourself the time to meditate, go for a walk, have some time to journal write, or even go to the spa. This is the first step of mindfulness training and one of the most important steps in grief healing. This is the time for you to be gentle with yourself. Sometimes even this step can be difficult to achieve; however, if this is all you do, CONGRATULATIONS! Celebrate the fact that you are taking time for yourself. Allow yourself to breathe. Most of the writing prompts in this book are influenced by self-care concepts which will help you through the second step of training, self-reflection.

The second step is **Self-Reflection**: Understand where you are in life and what your thoughts, feelings, and emotions are at this moment. Keep a few journals around your home and one in your car. Waves of grief can arise at anytime, and writing can help you move those emotions through you. Acknowledging the latter is extremely important, whether it is a positive or negative feeling in the moment, is crucial. We should not suppress any feelings we have in life. This is unhealthy for our physical and psychological wellbeing. The more you write your reflections, the more you are able to "ride the wave" and let them pass in a healthy manner.

The third step is **Self-Actualization**: By achieving the first two steps, you can then decide how to best move forward along your path and create a new normal in life. This stage happens when clarity sets in. New ideas may spark, or new goals may surface, helping you feel excited again in life. When we start to recognize and understand our feelings and emotions in the moment we can begin to experience growth and feel more fulfilled. By working through all three of these steps we are then able to achieve an optimal level of growth, our highest level of potential, and achieve our own greatness.

How we can use mindfulness in our life after loss?

There are many different ways we can incorporate mindfulness strategies into our day to day life. From simple breathing techniques, practicing meditation, taking a nature walk, to grabbing a marker and enjoying a moment of colouring. It's best to find out what you like to do and go from there. This is part of the deep listening piece of step one (self-care).

Another area is journal writing or guided writing. Many of us haven't thought about this fundamental skill since we were in grade school. As a former primary teacher, I understand the reasoning behind why we teach primary students how to journal write. If you have, what I call, a grief wave, allow these words, thoughts, and emotional feelings to flow through your mind and out onto paper. This is an amazing process to help you experince a mindfulness moment and release the emotions you are feeling more easily.

A grief wave is when, at any given moment, you think about the loss and, from deep inside of you, you can feel the emotions rising up and flushing out. This can be in the form of tears, anger, or even whaling out in an emotional response. I remember walking from my living room (about three months after my husband had passed) to the kitchen and felt these waves come from deep inside me, I fell to the kitchen floor and screamed out in disbelief "I can't believe you are gone". These moments are difficult, yet it is important to work through them rather than bottle them up deep inside and suppress them.

When writing out these daily writing prompts, I encourage you to focus on your thoughts and emotions. When I was teaching my students, I encouraged them not to worry about "speling", penmanship, or proper grammar (those were other lessons taught). These journal moments are merely to establish emotion-to-thought-to-word-to-writing techniques and to allow whatever is in your mind to flow up and out onto the surface on the paper. This is why I call it a wave, and you can "ride the wave" in this exercise. Whether or not the words are positive or negative, you are moving your thoughts and feelings towards self-reflection and self-actualization, helping you gain clarity again in your day to day life.

For example, this is why I had journals all over the house. I would be doing some housework and then a grief wave would happen, again I would think to myself, "I can't believe you are gone". What I figured out was if I could immediately put pen to paper and write, I would get my feelings out. The waves would come and flow through, and I would be able to continue on with my day. Yes tears would flow, but this process helped me move forward along my path. Day to day life began to get a bit easier, and I could start putting back my life, one puzzle piece at a time.

This guide is designed to help support you in this fundamental skill. Little prompts at the beginning of every page help you through the three steps I have outlined in the previous pages. Let the words flow for you to recognize your true being. The first couple of days it may only be a few words or how you are feeling. That is okay! There is no right or wrong way of completing these guided exercises. As I have previously mentioned, grief is different for all of us! This book is designed for you to develop a strong pattern along your path of self-discovery. The intention of writing is to discover who you are at your core and what you are mindful of throughout the days as the grief waves are flowing through. As you are completing this book, pay attention to the changes in your mindfulness writing. Measuring growth is important for the self-actualization component in mindfulness training.

Happy writing!

Welcome to mindfulness writing. I encourage you to do a daily guided entry. You may find yourself getting stronger in your mindfulness writing as the days unfold. If you miss a day or two, not to worry, just pick up where you left off. Guided writing is based on your soul's growth, rather then a calendar. Enjoy! There is also a notes section at the end of the book for you to write whenever you have those grief waves and need to release those emotions. We will begin easy and I will guide you in steps to build in mindfulness practice.

Breathing

We will begin with some breathing. One of the pieces of writing I found was from a Buddhist monk and his teachings to a student. The student asked why we practice the breath first? His response, he said the breath is the constant denominator in our life. Our breath doesn't change from the day we begin life to the day we transition onto the next realm. We can focus on our breath as something that doesn't change. This helps us understand that while other things around us change everyday (including loss), we can go back to the one thing that doesn't change. So let us begin with our breathing. Describe your breath.

_____
_____
_____
_____
_____
_____
_____
_____

Breathing

Breathing is highly important through grief waves and also with other symptoms that can be linked to loss as well. With your pen and journal in front of you, inhale for two, three, or four seconds. Exhale for two, three, or four seconds. Repeat a couple of times. Allow each breath to go deeper in the abdomen. Allow yourself to concentrate on the breath for these four second moments. When you feel ready, share your thoughts, words and feelings from your breathing exercise. Let these words flow...

Breathing

Let's continue the breathing exercise for the next couple of days. Allow five minutes everyday to focus on your breathing. If you need more space to write, please go to the back of the book. We will be building from this exercise, but for now, it is important to enjoy this moment of breathing, and listening to what your body is telling you. Write down your thoughts.

Breathing

Breathing...inhale, exhale, take these moments to enjoy the present moment. As you are breathing, what are you listening to? Notice how you are feeling and what your body needs at this time. It may need some extra water, or protein, or even extra sleep. Allow yourself to develop this listening skill from deep within. Being gentle during this time is highly important as you are moving forward. Allow yourself to acknowledge what it is you need. Share your thoughts.

Breathing

Breathing...listening... Congratulations! You are building the stepping stones for grief healing. Remember to continue these prompts at the back of the book if you need it. We can all respect that grief healing takes time, please continue writing and reflection based on the breath.

Daily Schedule

These next steps may sound easy or simple, but I encourage you, over the next 14 days to practice this writing prompt. Some of you may have difficulty waking up in the morning, which I know I did. However, keeping a daily agenda of your activities will help you continue to move forward along your path. Please allow yourself to write down everything you are doing and give yourself a check-mark when you are done. We are going to continue this for a week, however I encourage you to find another space (or even space at the back of the book) to continue with this routine. Even indulge yourself and go out to your local bookstore and purchase a brand new agenda. Celebrating the small accomplishments in your day help spark those "feel-good" moments. Big or small, these are amazing action moments we need to be proud of.

Here is an example from one of my first days after loss and how I completed this exercise. Please notice how it's simple and some days I didn't do much more than the basics. But I did it! I found reasons to get out of bed and every time I completed these tasks, I checked them off. You will notice the more you do this, the more your days will eventually fill up again with more magical events in your life.

Sample Daily Schedule
7:00 AM - wake up, feed the pups and pour myself a cup of coffee ✓
8:00 AM - breakfast and then hit the gym for some stretching ✓
9:00 AM
10:00 AM - come home for a snack and walk the pups ✓
11:00 AM
12:00 PM - eat lunch ✓
1:00 PM - meditate or bath time or go to the trails for a hike ✓
2:00 PM
3:00 PM - snack time and enjoy a cup of tea ✓
4:00 PM
5:00 PM - prep dinner ✓
6:00 PM
7:00 PM - retreat to the bedroom for some TV ✓

Daily Agenda

6:00 AM
7:00 AM
8:00 AM
9:00 AM
10:00 AM
11:00 AM
12:00 PM
1:00 PM
2:00 PM
3:00 PM
4:00 PM
5:00 PM
6:00 PM
7:00 PM
8:00 PM
9:00 PM
10:00 PM

Today's Reflections

Daily Agenda

6:00 AM
7:00 AM
8:00 AM
9:00 AM
10:00 AM
11:00 AM
12:00 PM
1:00 PM
2:00 PM
3:00 PM
4:00 PM
5:00 PM
6:00 PM
7:00 PM
8:00 PM
9:00 PM
10:00 PM

Today's Reflections

My Grieving Guide · The Mindful Way to Create Your New Normal

Daily Agenda

6:00 AM
7:00 AM
8:00 AM
9:00 AM
10:00 AM
11:00 AM
12:00 PM
1:00 PM
2:00 PM
3:00 PM
4:00 PM
5:00 PM
6:00 PM
7:00 PM
8:00 PM
9:00 PM
10:00 PM

Today's Reflections

Daily Agenda

6:00 AM
7:00 AM
8:00 AM
9:00 AM
10:00 AM
11:00 AM
12:00 PM
1:00 PM
2:00 PM
3:00 PM
4:00 PM
5:00 PM
6:00 PM
7:00 PM
8:00 PM
9:00 PM
10:00 PM

Today's Reflections

Daily Agenda

6:00 AM
7:00 AM
8:00 AM
9:00 AM
10:00 AM
11:00 AM
12:00 PM
1:00 PM
2:00 PM
3:00 PM
4:00 PM
5:00 PM
6:00 PM
7:00 PM
8:00 PM
9:00 PM
10:00 PM

Today's Reflections

Daily Agenda

6:00 AM
7:00 AM
8:00 AM
9:00 AM
10:00 AM
11:00 AM
12:00 PM
1:00 PM
2:00 PM
3:00 PM
4:00 PM
5:00 PM
6:00 PM
7:00 PM
8:00 PM
9:00 PM
10:00 PM

Today's Reflections

Daily Agenda

6:00 AM

7:00 AM

8:00 AM

9:00 AM

10:00 AM

11:00 AM

12:00 PM

1:00 PM

2:00 PM

3:00 PM

4:00 PM

5:00 PM

6:00 PM

7:00 PM

8:00 PM

9:00 PM

10:00 PM

Today's Reflections

Daily Agenda

6:00 AM
7:00 AM
8:00 AM
9:00 AM
10:00 AM
11:00 AM
12:00 PM
1:00 PM
2:00 PM
3:00 PM
4:00 PM
5:00 PM
6:00 PM
7:00 PM
8:00 PM
9:00 PM
10:00 PM

Today's Reflections

Daily Agenda

6:00 AM
7:00 AM
8:00 AM
9:00 AM
10:00 AM
11:00 AM
12:00 PM
1:00 PM
2:00 PM
3:00 PM
4:00 PM
5:00 PM
6:00 PM
7:00 PM
8:00 PM
9:00 PM
10:00 PM

Today's Reflections

Daily Agenda

6:00 AM
7:00 AM
8:00 AM
9:00 AM
10:00 AM
11:00 AM
12:00 PM
1:00 PM
2:00 PM
3:00 PM
4:00 PM
5:00 PM
6:00 PM
7:00 PM
8:00 PM
9:00 PM
10:00 PM

Today's Reflections

Daily Agenda

6:00 AM
7:00 AM
8:00 AM
9:00 AM
10:00 AM
11:00 AM
12:00 PM
1:00 PM
2:00 PM
3:00 PM
4:00 PM
5:00 PM
6:00 PM
7:00 PM
8:00 PM
9:00 PM
10:00 PM

Today's Reflections

Daily Agenda

6:00 AM
7:00 AM
8:00 AM
9:00 AM
10:00 AM
11:00 AM
12:00 PM
1:00 PM
2:00 PM
3:00 PM
4:00 PM
5:00 PM
6:00 PM
7:00 PM
8:00 PM
9:00 PM
10:00 PM

Today's Reflections

Daily Agenda

6:00 AM

7:00 AM

8:00 AM

9:00 AM

10:00 AM

11:00 AM

12:00 PM

1:00 PM

2:00 PM

3:00 PM

4:00 PM

5:00 PM

6:00 PM

7:00 PM

8:00 PM

9:00 PM

10:00 PM

Today's Reflections

Daily Agenda

6:00 AM
7:00 AM
8:00 AM
9:00 AM
10:00 AM
11:00 AM
12:00 PM
1:00 PM
2:00 PM
3:00 PM
4:00 PM
5:00 PM
6:00 PM
7:00 PM
8:00 PM
9:00 PM
10:00 PM

Today's Reflections

Let Us Recap!

Congratulations! Let us celebrate these steps for you moving forward. It's not easy and can I appreciate what you might be feeling. I hope that each day is getting easier for you. One step at a time. Let us take a moment and reflect on these past two exercises now. Spend some time doing your breathing routine and listening to your thoughts. You may want to include this exercise in your daily agenda. Whatever they are (positive or negative) write them down here. I encourage you to ask yourself, "what is something I have learned about myself in these past couple of weeks?" I've provided you with a few pages to reflect a bit deeper.

Let us continue to build...

One of the important messages I can not stress enough is the significant relationship we (as individuals) have with nature. Nature energy provides an abundance of healing and carries its own mindfulness training experiences simply by taking a walk along a wooded path. Forest bathing has become a popular mindfulness training tool around the world. Even through my own grief healing, I would head to the woods 4-5 days a week for at least 30 minutes of light walking to find clarity. There were days I would take my pups as well, and I noticed a huge difference in their behaviours after spending time in the forest. They were more calm, and less anxious on those days during the healing period. I noticed them happy, with their tails wagging. They were fully present, and it was amazing to see them enjoy that experience with me in the woods. These next set of reflection pages will help you find some calm moments. I recommend not using ear buds when walking, enjoy the nature sounds around you. Notice the birds or small critters in their element.

Happy trails!

Early Reflections

Take time in your space to reflect on your thoughts around nature. Use your breathing to help you become present in the moment. You may want to answer some of these questions: Have you ever been hiking before? Where do you like to go? Is the path by a lake or river, or in the woods? Write down your plan for walking in the woods.

Nature Walk

The leaves are calling me. I hear the sounds of the leaves rustling in the wind. I used to venture out onto the path many times during the week. The land represents the journey of an individual; there is a strong relationship between the path, the human, and personal growth. There are many twists and turns along the trail which can provide great wisdom. How was your first time out on the trails? Breath and share your thoughts.

Nature Walk and Breathing

Let us combine exercises now. Find a nature path you can go to for some enjoyment. Before stepping out onto the path, allow time to do your breathing exercise (from day one). Notice what kind of feelings you may have in those moments. How do you feel?

Gaia

Venture out onto the trails. Become mindful of your breathing and take in the sights, sounds, and smells of your surroundings. Feel the energy coming from Gaia (Mother Earth). She is there with you. She holds the ground strong for you to walk on, and she gives you that breath of fresh air. Notice the path: Is it straight? Is it curved? Are there any branches sticking out in which you may have to step over? Reflect and allow yourself to feel the strength coming from the path. Did you know that this is called "Forest Bathing"?

Gaia Exercise

Allow yourself to enjoy this exercise for three more days. You may wish to go to the same trail, you may wish to try different trails. Like every grief journey, preference will be different. And this is okay!

And the mindfulness continues...

Over the next set of guided writing prompts, they will look a little different each day. As you are building from past experiences, if you like one, I encourage you to continue with breathing, agenda setting, and nature hiking, all of these are for you to continue to build your new normal. In this space, I would like you to reflect on these building blocks. **What are** some things you are learning about yourself?

The Web

A spider spins it web through the night. She rebuilds reluctantly and effortlessly. Only to have what she has created, destroyed the next day by unforeseen forces. She, instinctively, continues again to rebuild. We can learn so much from the animal world. I have always been fascinated with spiders and how they beautifully weave their webs together in a perfect form of art. They rebuild and create if destroyed. So can we. Let us spend some time creating or colouring and instinctively move our pencil or pencil crayon from one space to another. You may want to purchase or find some adult colouring books which are a great idea for a mindfulness exercise. In the mean time, use these lines to reflect on how you are feeling today.

_____
_____
_____
_____
_____
_____
_____
_____
_____
_____
_____
_____
_____
_____
_____
_____
_____
_____

Darkness

The teachings from the west provide us with the understanding that in darkness is where we can find our own light along our path. Today I would like you to light a candle. Let this represent the light that is within you. As you are remembering your breathing, let your mind and your body enjoy the ambiance of this candle when you are writing.

Favourite Space

Spend some time and create (if you haven't done so already) a favourite reading nook or space. Make this your space, a place where you can feel comfortable, cozy, and have the ability to snuggle up and read a good book. Pick your favourite chair, couch, or space in your home. Allow yourself to breathe for a few moments and enjoy the sense of your space. This is an experience where you can observe all the beautiful things this space creates for you. Share what you are grateful for in this space.

_____
_____
_____
_____
_____
_____
_____
_____
_____
_____
_____
_____
_____
_____
_____
_____
_____
_____
_____
_____
_____

Words of Affirmation

One of the things I appreciated was when people would ask me "how are you doing TODAY?" Some questions can trigger anger or frustration, while others can warm your heart. Pay attention to the questions you like to hear from others. Write them down here - you may wish to share these with your friends and family so that they may be able to help you through these tougher days.

Zen

Finding your centre-being through breathing is a great mindfulness practice. Take a few moments (you can even put on some meditation music) and enjoy inhaling, visualizing the breath going straight to your heart-centre of your being. Enjoy the next 5-10 minutes. Let this be called "centering". Share your reflections. Congratulations... we are moving into the physical component of mindfulness training.

Mindfulness Body

As we continue to build our new normal we will add in some additional threads, helping you along your path. Now we are able to bring together mindfulness training and the physical body. Working out is a great way to stay balanced and helps you sift through those emotions from deep within and move them out in a healthy manner. Working out does not have to be strenuous. You may want to take up a new yoga or stretching class, or join a running club. Whatever your physical capabilities are, enjoy looking at working out in a new mindfulness way.

The Body

Working out is an amazing healthy habit. Even though you may feel sluggish during these difficult times, I found it helpful to go to the gym to simply stretch. It gave me the opportunity to get out, have a change of pace, and focus on my physical body. A workout can be as light as walking your dog, or more advanced like going to the gym for a high intensity interval training class. Whatever your level is for active healthy living, today I would like for you to enjoy your post-workout time by writing about how you are feeling.

Agenda

Let us go back to the agenda example and see where we can now add in new workouts to our daily life. When do you like to workout? Is it in the morning before work? Or maybe you like to do it in the evening? Whatever the time of day is, scheduling it will help you keep focused. Write down your thoughts and plans.

Zen-ful

If you haven't done so already, I would like you to spend some time and add in at least three workouts a week as part of your weekly agenda routine. As you will notice, if you have kept up with the agenda exercise, adding in more activities will help you build that new lifestyle you are working towards. What are your plans for exercise? They can be as simple as walking the dog, or as "zen-ful" as yoga and stretching. We will focus on working out for the next seven days.

Workout Reflections

Workout Reflections

Workout Reflections

Workout Reflections

Workout Reflections

Workout Reflections

Workout Reflections

Weaving and Reflecting

As we weave these three components together, you will be able to build mindfulness training into your life. Weaving these tools together reminds us of the sweet grass braid. Each strand separately, will break. Yet when they come together and are braided, they become an unbreakable force. By practicing these fundamentals, they are helping you build strength, confidence, and are providing you with the clarity you need to continue moving forward along your path. So let us reflect on these preliminary steps:

The preliminary steps of breathing will help assist you in moving through those grief waves. Agenda setting will help you continue to realize that life continues to move forward for you in these moments of trials and tribulations. They aren't easy by any means. The breath reminds us that it is the only constant thing in life. We are given breath when we are first born and it is the only thing in life that continues until we are ready to move into the next realm. These teachings have stemmed from indigenous and Buddhist elders who helped me to remember my breathing when life gets rough and the grief fog sets in.

The next stage in this book has you establish an agenda strategy. This helps you find purpose to get up in the morning if you find it difficult after your loss.

The third step (linking to additional strands like nature) is establishing exercise routines. Like I said, they don't have to be overly strenuous, but focusing on the physical body helps alleviate the pressures from the emotional and psychological states of grief. Even something light, go for a walk, enjoy the trails, or find a gym to enjoy these amazing moments of loving yourself as you continue to heal.

Much like the sweet grass braid, weaving together these fundamentals builds the strength for you to achieve your goals and dreams in life. And like I mentioned before, each strand within the braid, if it were to stand on its own, would break. Yet by weaving together the strands, your braid becomes a force!

Gratitude

Practicing gratitude is an amazing mindfulness tool to help you appreciate life's magical moments. You can build upon these feelings of gratitude with new ideas you wish to do while moving forward along your path. Have you ever wanted to take up a cooking class? Or try a new yoga class? Have you ever wanted to take up art? Over the next seven days, we are going to continue building our writing skills by thinking of the things we are grateful for. Each day I would like you to write down three things you are grateful for. They can be as small as showing gratitude for a cup of tea, or as significant as receiving a gift. Now write down some ideas you may have for things you would like to manifest in life (big or small). This exercise can be quite powerful. There is space for you to write your daily reflections as well.

Gratitude

Things I am grateful for are...

1

2

3

Things I wish to create in life are...

1

2

3

Gratitude

Things I am grateful for are...

1 _____

2 _____

3 _____

Things I wish to create in life are...

1 _____

2 _____

3 _____

Daily Reflections

_____

_____

_____

_____

_____

_____

_____

Gratitude

Things I am grateful for are...

1 _____

2 _____

3 _____

Things I wish to create in life are...

1 _____

2 _____

3 _____

Daily Reflections

_____
_____
_____
_____
_____
_____
_____
_____

Gratitude

Things I am grateful for are...

1

2

3

Things I wish to create in life are...

1

2

3

Daily Reflections

Gratitude

Things I am grateful for are...

1

2

3

Things I wish to create in life are...

1

2

3

Daily Reflections

Gratitude

Things I am grateful for are...

1

2

3

Things I wish to create in life are...

1

2

3

Daily Reflections

Gratitude

Things I am grateful for are...

1

2

3

Things I wish to create in life are...

1

2

3

Daily Reflections

Gratitude

Things I am grateful for are...

1

2

3

Things I wish to create in life are...

1

2

3

Daily Reflections

Self-Care Writing Prompts

Sometimes we find it difficult to allow ourselves those opportunities of self-care. These next prompts are to help you find time for self-care and create exercises where you can find ones that you enjoy and continue to help you reflect. I encourage you to try them all and pay attention to the ones you prefer. If it's adult colouring you like, then spend more of your self-care time in the future colouring.

Musical Notes

Music's vibrational frequencies help spark creativity for us. From meditation music, holiday, country, pop, rock, all of these carry with them sound waves to help us grow and expand. What is your favourite music to listen to when you are creative in life? What are the sounds? What feelings surface when you listen? Does it make you want to dance or meditate?

Pay it Forward

Reciprocity makes it possible to build continuing relationships and exchanges through positive interactions. It is about the unconditional act of social gift-giving without any hope or expectation of future positive responses. Have you ever experienced a "pay it forward" event?

Little Toy Trains

Creating and learning also enhances your sensory skills, as sensory play is essential for childhood brain development. Play helps children develop and make sense of their relationships to the world around them. They help create mindfulness moments when we are deep in this type of play. What was your favourite toy as a child? Share your memories.

Tasty Treat

Treat day! We can all indulge from time to time. Take a piece of chocolate (light, medium, or dark) and enjoy the tasty sensation! Let it sit in your mouth and feel it melting. Share your experience. If you don't have a sweet tooth, enjoy something salty or pick a favourite snack. If it's chocolate you are enjoying, please refrain from over-indulging every day. Allow yourself a treat day once a week. Maintaining a balance is key!

Colour Wonder

Adult colouring came into popularity a couple of years ago. Why? Well human beings naturally look for alternative ways to improve their mindfulness skills. Adult colouring brings them back to their childhood which help create an inner child wonder about them. Today I encourage you to do some colouring then reflect on your experience.

Bath Time

Have you ever indulged in a self care bath? Epsom salts, essential oils, a candle, or maybe even some relaxation music? Or do you like bubbles? Enjoy your bath and then write about your experience.

Pen and Quill

When do you like to write? Is it in the morning? Is it in the evening after your day? Share your thoughts about today (or previous day) and the events that led up to yourself in this moment. What are you most grateful for?

Reflections

Goal setting is important for us human beings to grow, expand, and create along our path. After these writing prompts, do you have some new ideas you wish to do or achieve now moving forward? Would you like to take a new culinary class? Or maybe go on a new trip or adventure? Write down two dreams you have had lately and begin the process of making them become goals you wish to work towards.

Enjoyment

Mindfulness practice is more than meditation. More studies have been done to find many wonderful activities for people to enhance their mindfulness training. From colouring, to reading, or enjoying time with your pet, studies have shown these are as effective as meditation. After these past guided writing prompts, what is something that you enjoying doing more than others?

Conclusions and Final Notes

Congratulations and I hope you enjoyed your mindfulness experiences. I encourage you to continue building your "new normal". Remember, we all walk the path of grief differently. I hope this guide has helped you discover more about yourself and what you enjoy doing moving forward along your path. The intention was to create ideas and have you weave them together to get you started on building your new life.

Whether you are in a state of complete joy in life, or you may have encountered some trials and tribulations, guided writing is a highly effective tool for you to experience. I hope you have taken the time to evaluate yourself between the sections. Measuring growth along your path is also important to help you get to where you want to be in life. Thank you again and I wish you many blessings along your path.

With Much Love,
JenCB

Notes:

Notes:

Notes:

Notes:

Notes:

Notes:

Notes:

Notes:

Notes:

Notes:

Notes:

Notes:

Notes:

Notes:

Notes:

Notes:

Notes:

Notes:

Notes:

Notes:

Notes:

References

Campbell, S. (2006). *Layers of place in Interdisciplinary studies in literature and environment*: ISLE. 13(2), pp. 179-183 Indiana University of Pennsylvania

Coles, T (2017). *Forests Schools, In Canada, What Are They, and What Are the Benefits?* Retrieved from: https://www.huffingtonpost.ca/2017/09/29/forest-schools-canada_a_23227782/

Dispenza, J. (2014) *You Are The Placebo*. Hay House. USA

Kabatt-Zinn, J. (2017). *The Science of Mindfulness, Greater Good Science Centre*. Retrieved Nov. 5 from : Roemer, L., & Orsillo, S. M. (2002). Expanding our conceptualization of and treatment for General Anxiety Disorder: Integrating mindfulness/acceptance-based approaches with existing cognitive-behavioral models. Clinical Psychology: Science and Practice, 9, 27-44.

Kublar-Ross and Kelser (2005) *On Grief and Grieving*. Shimen and Shuster Inc. New York

Park, J. (2016) *When perceptions defy reality. The relationships between depression and actual and perceived social support.* Journal of Affective Disorders (200) : pp. 37-44

Praagh J., and Virtue, D. (2013). *How to heal a grieving heart*. Hay House Publications. U. S. A

Tolle, E. (1999). *The Power of Now*. Namaste Publishing. Canada

Williams, M. PhD (2014). *Follow the Shaman's Call*. Llewellyn Publications. Woodbury. MN

Wagamese, R. (2016). *Embers: One Ojibway's Meditations*. Douglas and MacIntyre. Canada.

Unknown Author. (2018). *Mindfulness defined*. Retrieved from: http. greatergoodmagazine.com